COUNTRIES OF THE WORLD

South Korea

by Bryan Langdo

BELLWETHER MEDIA • MINNEAPOLIS, MN

Blastoff! Readers are carefully developed by literacy experts to build reading stamina and move students toward fluency by combining standards-based content with developmentally appropriate text.

Level 1 provides the most support through repetition of high-frequency words, light text, predictable sentence patterns, and strong visual support.

Level 2 offers early readers a bit more challenge through varied sentences, increased text load, and text-supportive special features.

Level 3 advances early-fluent readers toward fluency through increased text load, less reliance on photos, advancing concepts, longer sentences, and more complex special features.

★ **Blastoff! Universe**

Reading Level

Grade K

Grades 1–3

Grade 4

This edition first published in 2025 by Bellwether Media, Inc.

No part of this publication may be reproduced in whole or in part without written permission of the publisher. For information regarding permission, write to Bellwether Media, Inc., Attention: Permissions Department, 6012 Blue Circle Drive, Minnetonka, MN 55343.

Library of Congress Cataloging-in-Publication Data

LC record for South Korea available at: https://lccn.loc.gov/2024012087

Text copyright © 2025 by Bellwether Media, Inc. BLASTOFF! READERS and associated logos are trademarks and/or registered trademarks of Bellwether Media, Inc. Bellwether Media is a division of Chrysalis Education Group.

Editor: Suzane Nguyen   Designer: Laura Sowers

Printed in the United States of America, North Mankato, MN.

Table of Contents

All About South Korea	4
Land and Animals	6
Life in South Korea	12
South Korea Facts	20
Glossary	22
To Learn More	23
Index	24

All About South Korea

Seoul

South Korea is in eastern Asia. It lies on a small **peninsula**. Seoul is the capital.

Pop music is big in South Korea. Many people love **K-pop**!

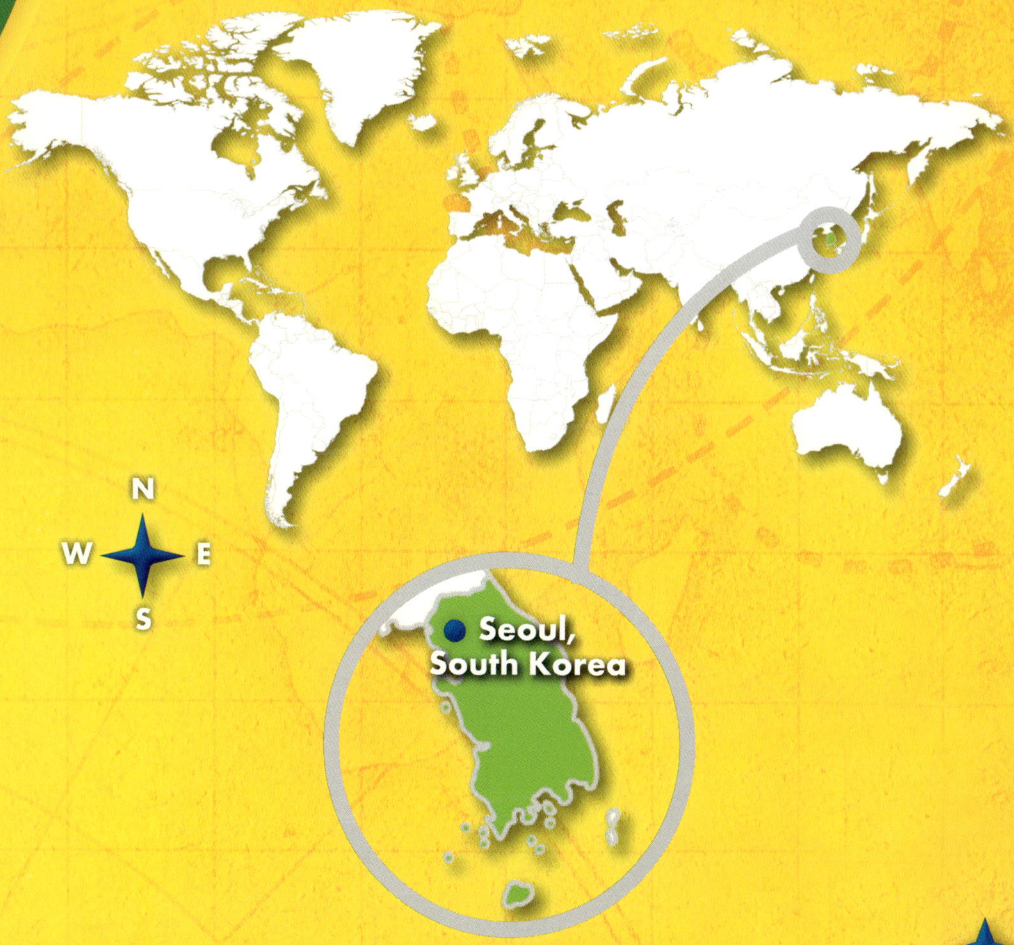

Land and Animals

Mountains cover most of South Korea. The Han River runs through Seoul.

The coast has many **inlets**. Thousands of islands lie off the coast.

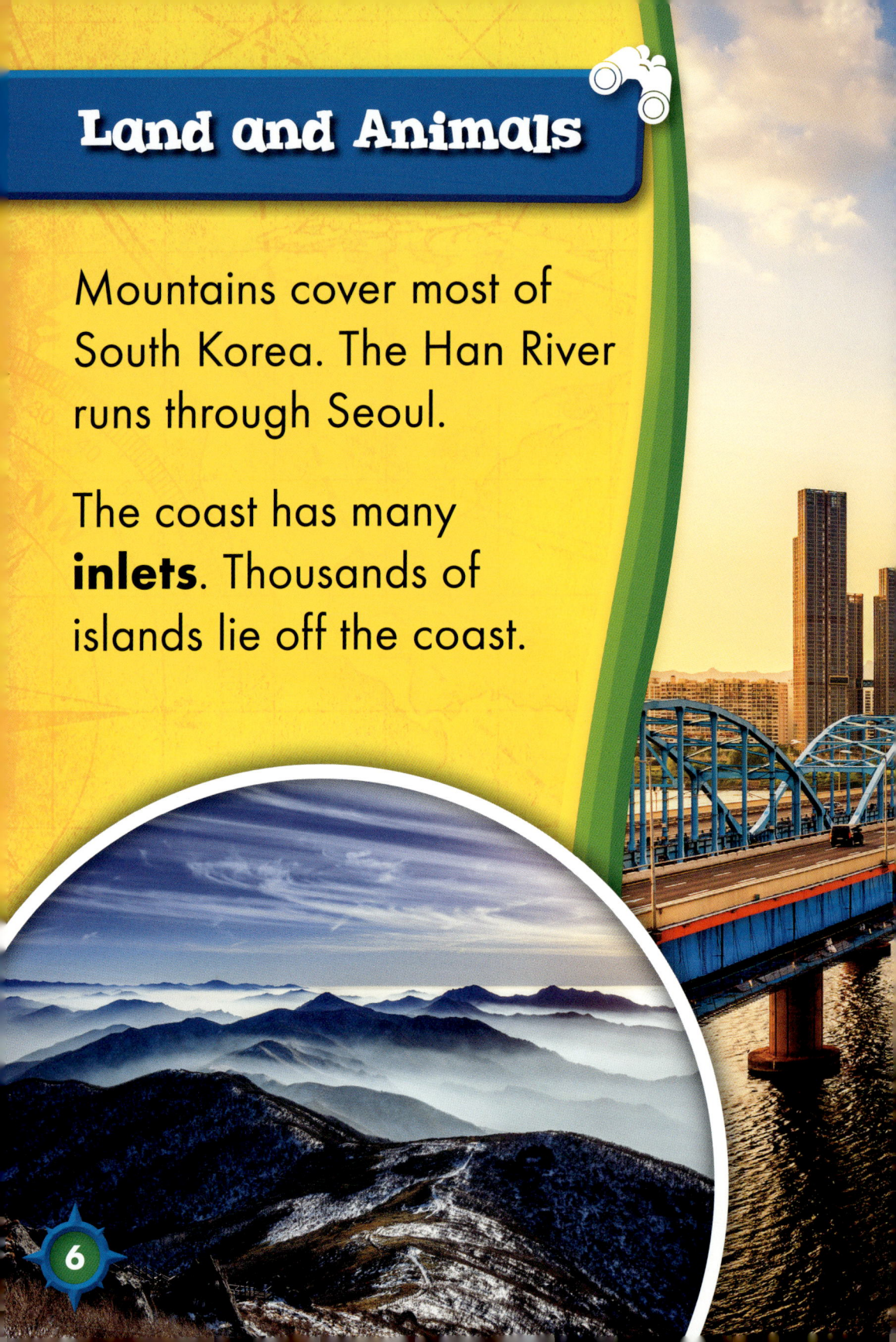

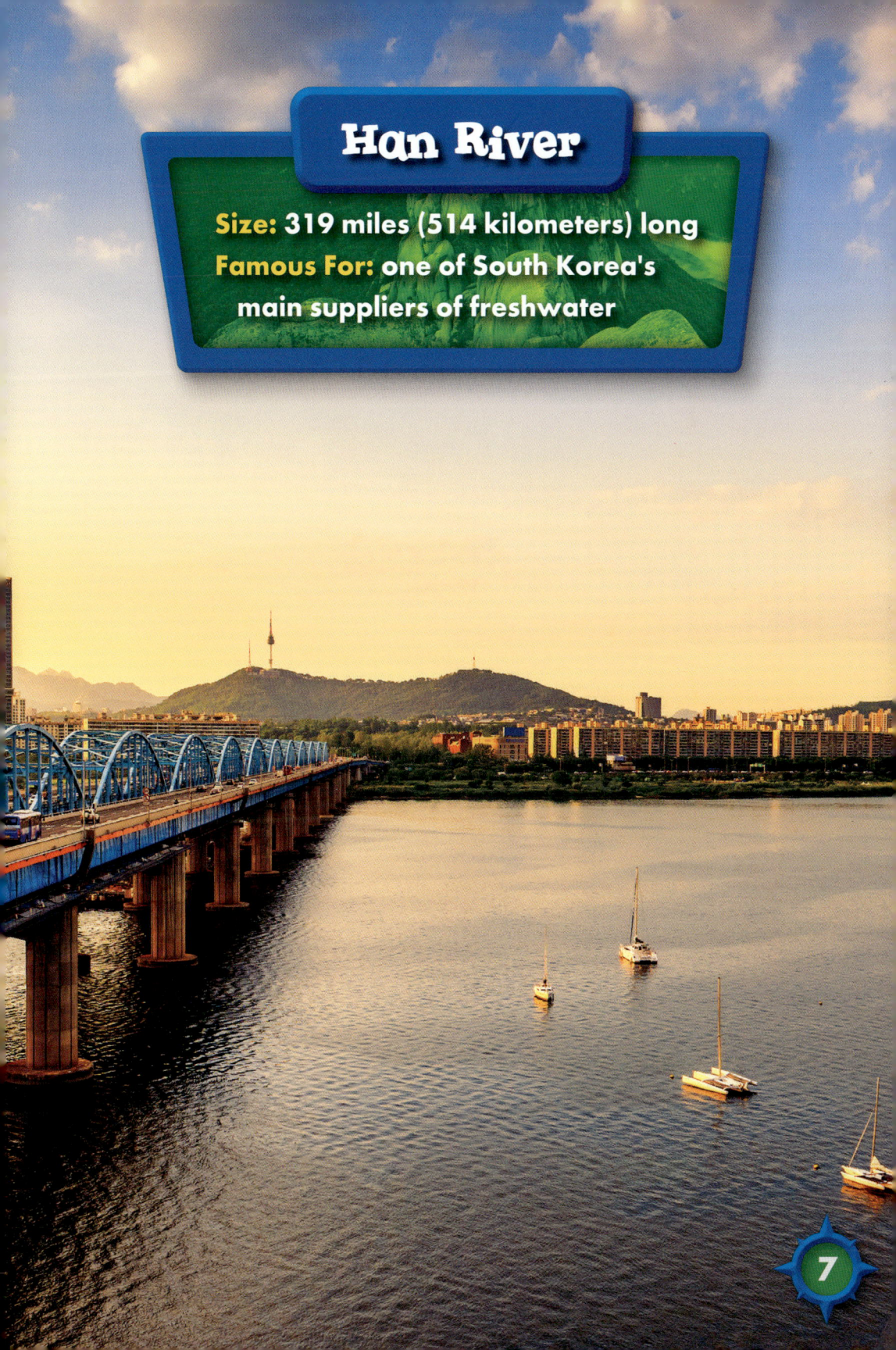

Han River

Size: 319 miles (514 kilometers) long
Famous For: one of South Korea's main suppliers of freshwater

summer

South Korea has cold winters. Summers are hot. The south is warmer than the north.

Monsoons happen every year. They bring a lot of rain.

Most animals live in **national parks**. Black bears climb trees. Magpies fly over treetops.

Asian magpie

Otters swim in rivers.
Water deer eat grass nearby.

Life in South Korea

Koreans are the main **ethnic** group. They speak Korean.

Most people live in cities. They live in apartments.

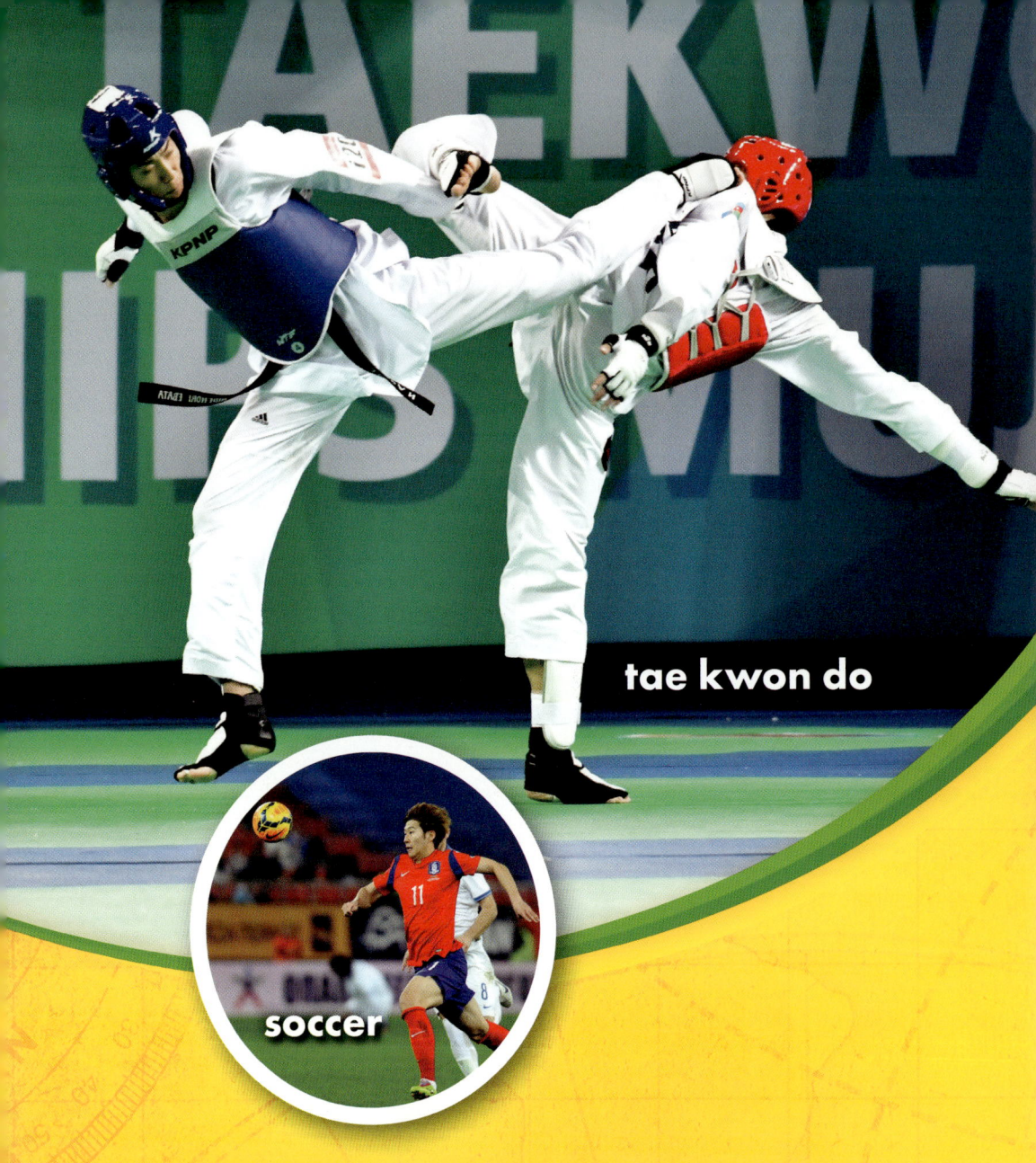

tae kwon do

soccer

People enjoy tae kwon do. It is a **martial art**. Baseball and soccer are also popular.

People hike in the mountains.
Many people play video games.

hiking

Kimchi is eaten at most meals. It is pickled vegetables. *Bibimbap* has rice and vegetables. It is topped with an egg.

Korean Foods

kimchi

bibimbap

japchae

bulgogi

Japchae is a noodle dish.
Bulgogi is grilled beef.

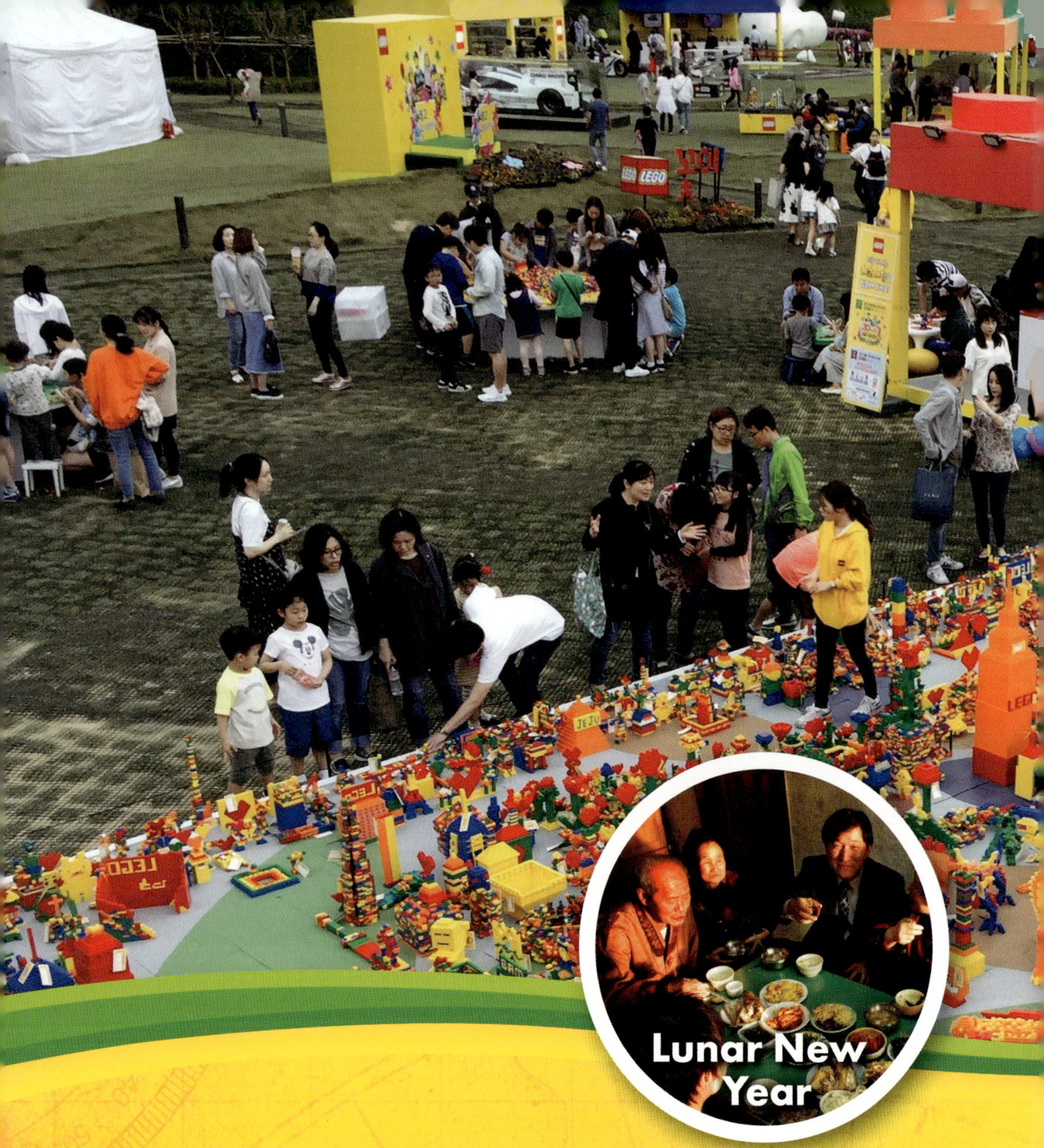

Lunar New Year

Lunar New Year is in the winter.
People eat with their families.

Children's Day

May 5 is Children's Day!
Parks are crowded with kids.
Koreans enjoy family time!

South Korea Facts

Size:
38,502 square miles (99,720 square kilometers)

Population:
51,966,948 (2023)

National Holiday:
National Liberation Day of Korea (August 15)

Main Language:
Korean

Capital City:
Seoul

Famous Face

Name: Jungkook

Famous For: a singer, rapper, and dancer who is a member of BTS, one of the most successful K-pop bands

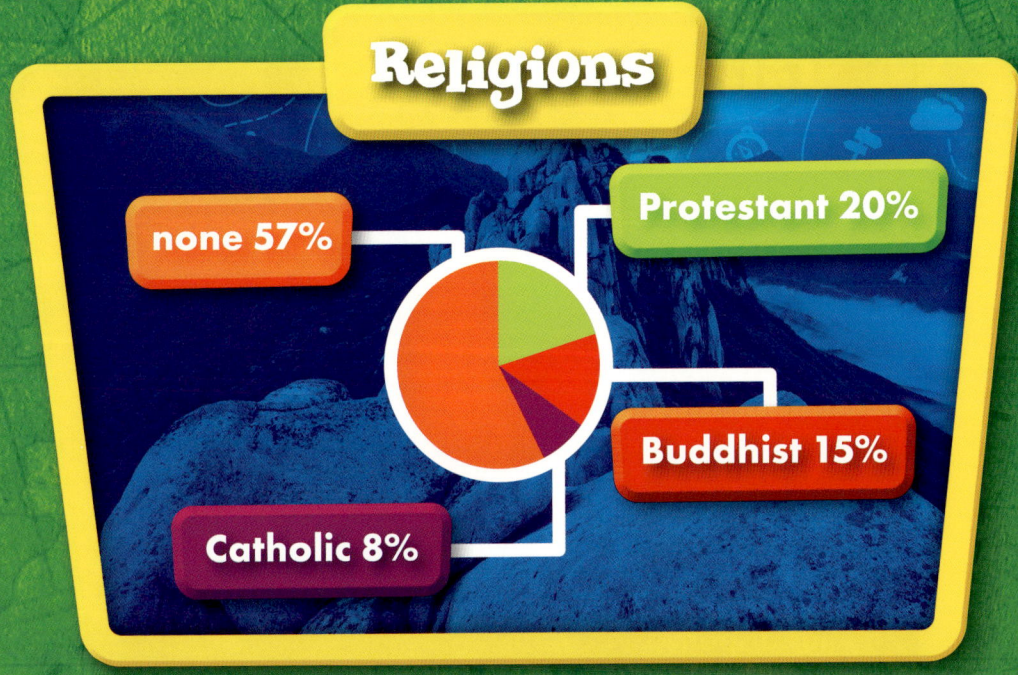

Religions

- none 57%
- Protestant 20%
- Buddhist 15%
- Catholic 8%

Top Landmarks

Bukchon Hanok Village

Gyeongbokgung Palace

Seoraksan National Park

Glossary

ethnic—related to races or large groups of people who share things such as customs, religion, and language

inlets—narrow bays; bays are small areas filled with ocean water.

K-pop—Korean pop music

lunar—related to the moon

martial art—any form of self-defense that is practiced as a sport

monsoons—winds that shift direction each season; monsoons bring heavy rain.

national parks—areas of land that a country sets aside for natural or historic reasons

peninsula—a section of land that sticks out from a larger piece of land and is almost completely surrounded by water

To Learn More

AT THE LIBRARY

Andrews, Elizabeth. *Jung Kook: BTS Singer and Beyond*. Minneapolis, Minn.: Pop!, 2024.

Pierce, Simon, and Laura L. Sullivan. *South Korea*. Buffalo, N.Y.: Cavendish Square Publishing, 2024.

Wood, John. *A Visit to South Korea*. Minneapolis, Minn.: Bearport Publishing, 2023.

ON THE WEB

FACTSURFER

Factsurfer.com gives you a safe, fun way to find more information.

1. Go to www.factsurfer.com.
2. Enter "South Korea" into the search box and click 🔍.
3. Select your book cover to see a list of related content.

Index

animals, 10, 11
apartments, 12
Asia, 4
baseball, 14
capital (see Seoul)
Children's Day, 19
cities, 12
coast, 6
food, 16, 17
Han River, 6, 7
hike, 15
inlets, 6
islands, 6
Korean, 12, 13
Lunar New Year, 18
map, 5
monsoons, 9
mountains, 6, 15
music, 5
national parks, 10
peninsula, 4

people, 5, 12, 14, 15, 18, 19
rain, 9
say hello, 13
Seoul, 4, 5, 6
soccer, 14
South Korea facts, 20–21
summers, 8
tae kwon do, 14
video games, 15
winters, 8, 18

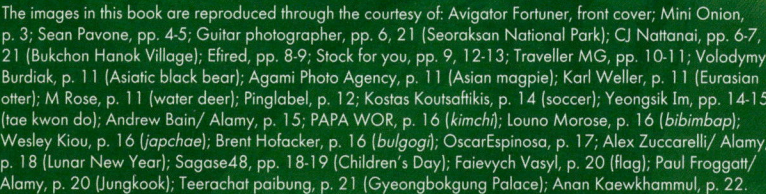

The images in this book are reproduced through the courtesy of: Avigator Fortuner, front cover; Mini Onion, p. 3; Sean Pavone, pp. 4-5; Guitar photographer, pp. 6, 21 (Seoraksan National Park); CJ Nattanai, pp. 6-7, 21 (Bukchon Hanok Village); Efired, pp. 8-9; Stock for you, pp. 9, 12-13; Traveller MG, pp. 10-11; Volodymyr Burdiak, p. 11 (Asiatic black bear); Agami Photo Agency, p. 11 (Asian magpie); Karl Weller, p. 11 (Eurasian otter); M Rose, p. 11 (water deer); Pinglabel, p. 12; Kostas Koutsaftikis, p. 14 (soccer); Yeongsik Im, pp. 14-15 (tae kwon do); Andrew Bain/ Alamy, p. 15; PAPA WOR, p. 16 (*kimchi*); Louno Morose, p. 16 (*bibimbap*); Wesley Kiou, p. 16 (*japchae*); Brent Hofacker, p. 16 (*bulgogi*); OscarEspinosa, p. 17; Alex Zuccarelli/ Alamy, p. 18 (Lunar New Year); Sagase48, pp. 18-19 (Children's Day); Faievych Vasyl, p. 20 (flag); Paul Froggatt/ Alamy, p. 20 (Jungkook); Teerachat paibung, p. 21 (Gyeongbokgung Palace); Anan Kaewkhammul, p. 22.